AARON COPLAND

Old American Songs
Complete

BOOSEY & HAWKES

DISTRIBUTED BY

7777 W. BLUEMOUND RD. P.O. BOX 13819 MILWAUKEE, WI 53213

www.boosey.com
www.halleonard.com

The first set of *Old American Songs* was completed in 1950, the same year that Copland finished his other major song set, *Twelve Poems of Emily Dickinson.* While Copland was writing the songs, tenor Peter Pears and composer Benjamin Britten came to visit him. Taken by Copland's new settings, they left with his promise of receiving copies of the songs in England to perform. On October 17, 1950, the first set was given its world premiere by Pears with Britten at the piano at their Aldeburgh Festival. The American premiere took place in New York on January 28, 1951, with Copland accompanying baritone William Warfield. The success of the first set prompted Copland to set five more songs. Finished in 1952, the second set was premiered by Warfield and Copland at the Castle Hill Concerts in Massachusetts on July 24 of that year. Copland would later orchestrate both sets for medium voice and small orchestra. Warfield sang the premiere of the orchestrated first set with the Los Angeles Philharmonic, conducted by Alfred Wallenstein, on January 7, 1955. Grace Bumbry premiered the second set with the Ojai Festival Orchestra on May 25, 1955, with Copland on the podium.

Contents

FIRST SET

1. *The Boatmen's Dance*
Published in Boston in 1843 as an "original banjo melody" by Old Dan. D. Emmett, who later composed *Dixie*. From the Harris Collection of American Poetry and Plays in Brown University.

2. *The Dodger*
As sung by Mrs. Emma Dusenberry of Mena, Arkansas, who learned it in the 1880's. Supposedly used in the Cleveland-Blaine presidential campaign. Published by John A. and Alan Lomax in *Our Singing Country*.

3. *Long Time Ago*
Issued in 1837 by George Pope Morris, who adapted the words, and Charles Edward Horn, who arranged the music from an anonymous, original minstrel tune. Also from the Harris Collection.

4. *Simple Gifts*
A favorite song of the Shaker sect, from the period 1837-1847. The melody and words were quoted by Edward D. Andrews in his book of Shaker rituals, songs and dances, entitled *The Gift To Be Simple*.

5. *I Bought Me a Cat*
A children's nonsense song. This version was sung to the composer by the American playwright Lynn Riggs, who learned it during his boyhood in Oklahoma.

SECOND SET

1. *The Little Horses*
A children's lullaby song originating in the Southern States – date unknown. This adaptation founded in part on John A. and Alan Lomax's version in *Folk Song U.S.A.*

2. *Zion's Walls*
A revivalist song. Original melody and words credited to John G. McCurry, compiler of the *Social Harp*. Published by George P. Jackson in *Down East Spirituals*.

3. *The Golden Willow Tree*
Variant of the well-known Anglo-American ballad, more usually called *The Golden Vanity*. This version is based on a recording issued by the Library of Congress Music Division from its collection of the Archive of American Folk Song. Justus Begley recorded it with banjo accompaniment for Alan and Elizabeth Lomax in 1937.

4. *At the River*
Hymn Tune. Words and melody are by Rev. Robert Lowry, 1865.

5. *Ching-a-ring Chaw*
Minstrel Song. The words have been adapted from the original, in the Harris Collection of American Poetry and Plays in Brown University.

Old American Songs

FIRST SET

1. THE BOATMEN'S DANCE

(Minstrel Song-1843)

original key: E Major

Arranged by
AARON COPLAND

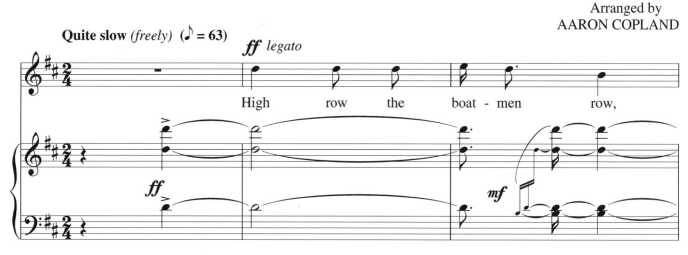

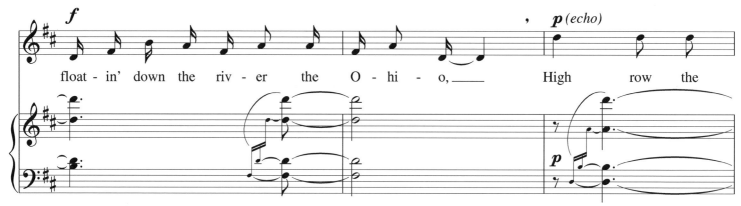

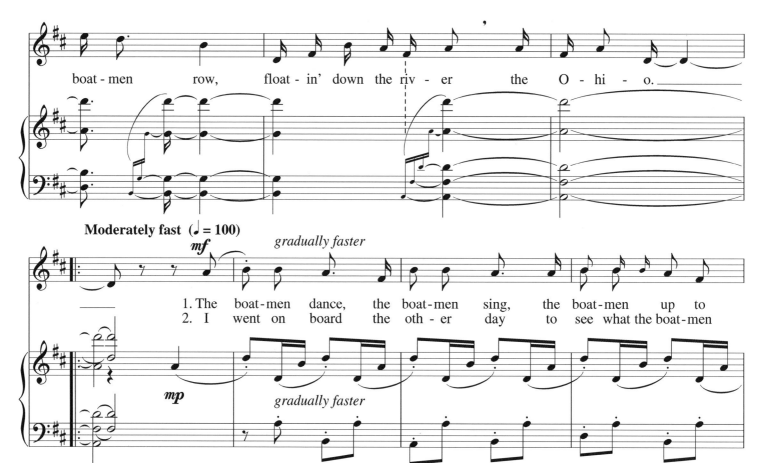

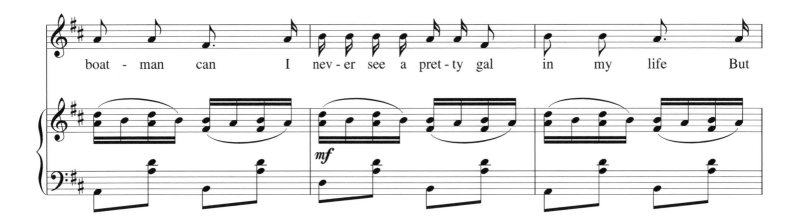

2. THE DODGER

(Campaign Song)

original key: G Major

Arranged by
AARON COPLAND

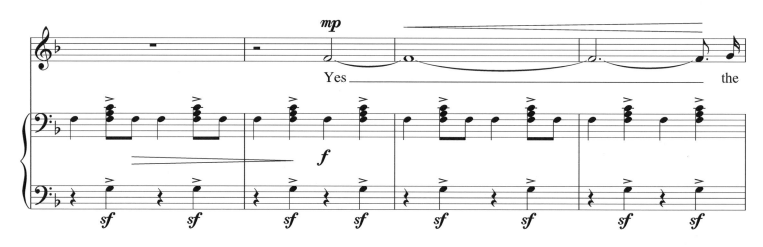

look out girls___ he's a-tell-in' you a lie Yes we're all

dodg - in', _____ a - dodg - in', dodg - in', dodg - in' Yes we're

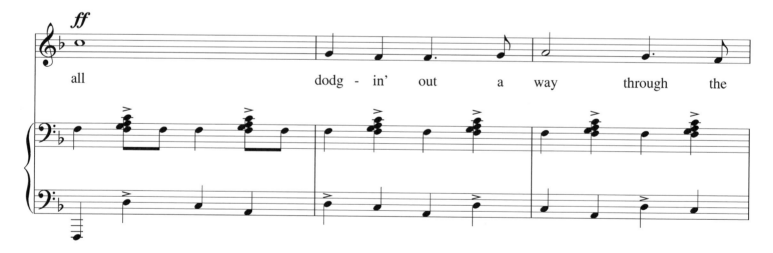

all dodg - in' out a way through the

world. _____

3. LONG TIME AGO
(Ballad)
original key: B♭ Major

Arranged by
AARON COPLAND

16

4. SIMPLE GIFTS

(Shaker Song)

original key: A♭ Major

Arranged by
AARON COPLAND

[2nd time to Coda]

love and de-light. _____ When true sim-pli-ci-ty is gained To

mf (plainly)

bow and to bend we shan't be a-shamed To turn, turn will be our de-light 'Till by

turn-ing, turn-ing we come round right. _____ 'Tis the

CODA

(dreamily)

5. I BOUGHT ME A CAT
(Children's Song)
original key: F Major

Arranged by
AARON COPLAND

22

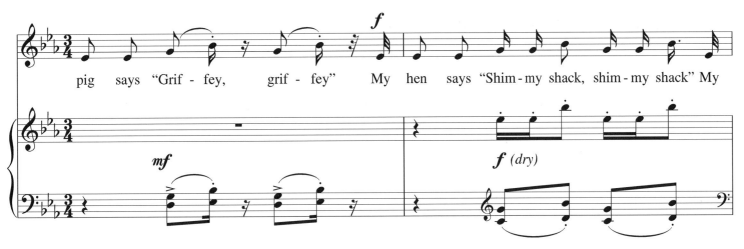

pig says "Grif - fey, grif - fey" My hen says "Shim - my shack, shim - my shack" My

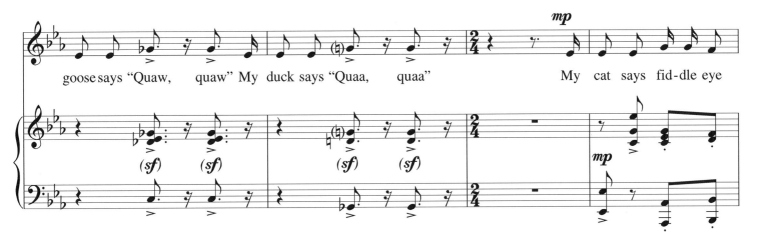

goose says "Quaw, quaw" My duck says "Quaa, quaa" My cat says fid - dle eye

fee. I bought me a cow My cow pleased me I fed my cow un - der

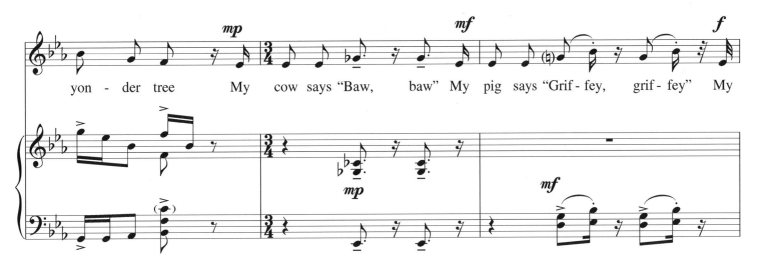

yon - der tree My cow says "Baw, baw" My pig says "Grif - fey, grif - fey" My

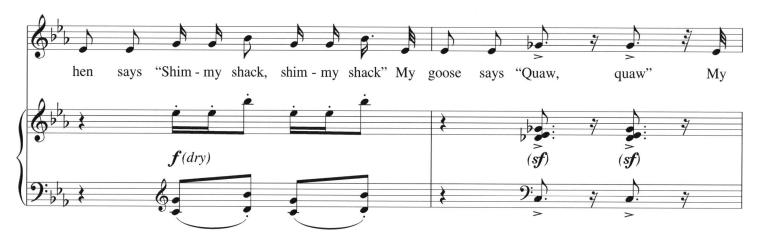

hen says "Shim - my shack, shim - my shack" My goose says "Quaw, quaw" My

duck says "Quaa, quaa" My cat says fid - dle eye fee. I

bought me a horse My horse pleased me I fed my horse un - der

yon - der tree My horse says "Neigh, neigh" My cow says "Baw, baw" My

pig says "Grif - fey, grif - fey" My hen says "Shim-my shack, shim-my shack" My

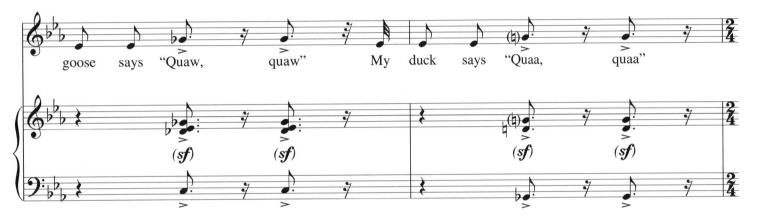

goose says "Quaw, quaw" My duck says "Quaa, quaa" My

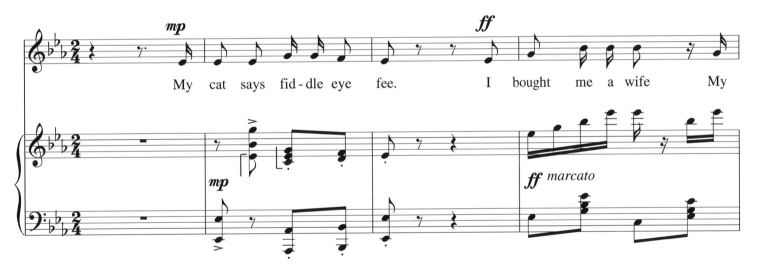

My cat says fid-dle eye fee. I bought me a wife My

wife pleased me I fed my wife un-der yon - der tree My

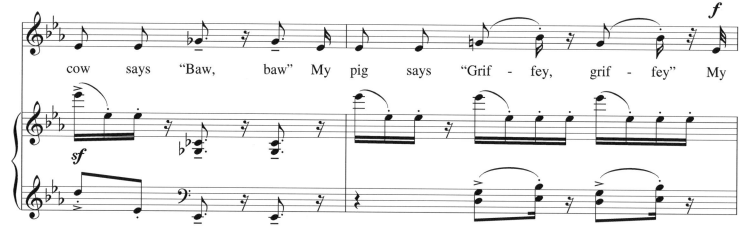

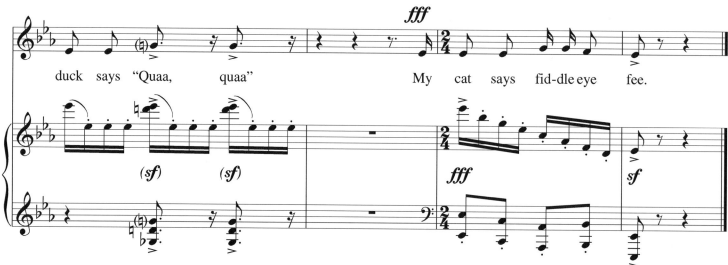

Old American Songs

SECOND SET

1. THE LITTLE HORSES
(Lullaby)
original key: E minor

Arranged by
AARON COPLAND

black and a bay and a brown and a gray and a Coach

(no ritard.)

più f

(long) *ad lib.* **As at first** *(slowly)* *p*

and six - a lit - tle hor - ses. Hush you bye,

a tempo *f* *mf* *p*

mp

Don't you cry, Oh you pret - ty lit - tle ba - by. Go to sleep - y lit - tle

mp

p poco ad lib.

ba - by. Oh you pret - ty lit - tle ba - by.

p *mp*

Ped. * Ped. *

2. ZION'S WALLS

(Revivalist Song)

original key: F Major

Arranged by
AARON COPLAND

With a moderate swing (♩. = 80)

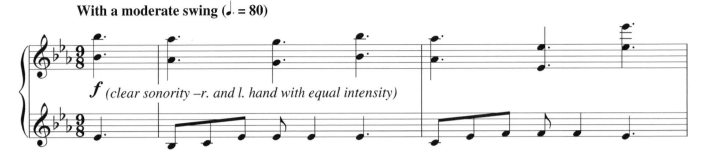

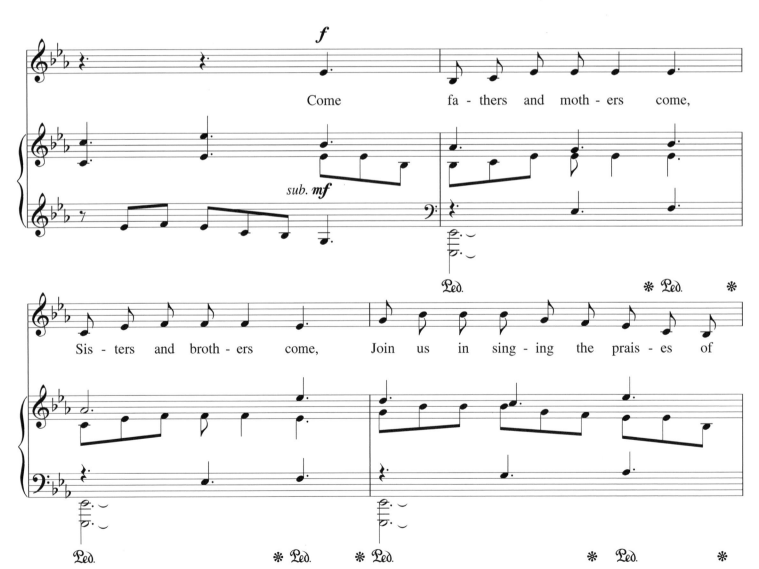

walls _ of Zi-on._____

senza Ped.

Ped.

f

Come fa - thers and moth - ers, Come

upper voice legato

mf

Ped.   * Ped. * Ped.   * Ped. *

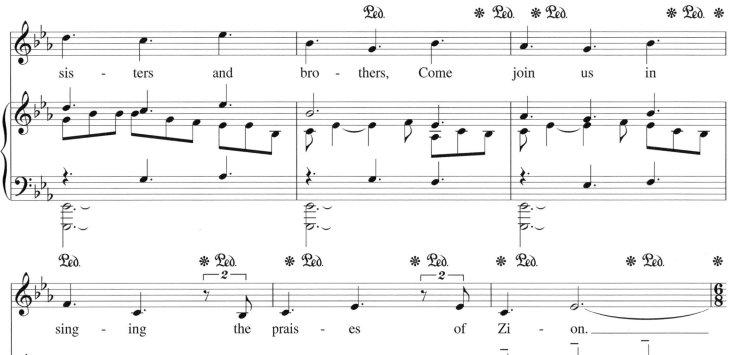

sis - ters and bro - thers, Come join us in

Ped.   * Ped.   * Ped.   * Ped.   * Ped.   * Ped.   *

sing - ing the prais - es of Zi - on._____

Ped.   * Ped.   *

feel de-ter-mined to meet_ with-in____ the walls_ of Zi - on, We'll

less loud   *gradually louder*

shout and go round, We'll shout and go round,_ We'll shout and go round, We'll

less loud   *gradually louder*

f louder

shout and go round_ the walls_ of Zi - on,_____ the walls_ of Zi - on,_____

f

ff

___ the walls_ of Zi - on._____

ff   *hold back*   *sff*

3. THE GOLDEN WILLOW TREE

(Anglo-American Ballad)

original key: G Major

Arranged by
AARON COPLAND

I'll give thee, _____ the _ fair-est of my daugh-ters as she

sails up - on the sea, If you'll sink 'em in the low -

- land lone-some low, If you'll sink 'em in the land that lies so

low." _____ He

turned up-on his back and a - way swum he, He__ swum till he came to the

8va

(r.h. glassy)

p

Brit - ish Ro - ver - ie, He had a lit - tle in - stru - ment fit - ted for his use, He__

(8)

bored nine holes and he bored them all at once. He turned up-on his breast and

(8)

loco

back swum he, He__ swum till he came to the Gold-en Wil-low Tree.

44

low, Though you sank 'em in the land that lies so

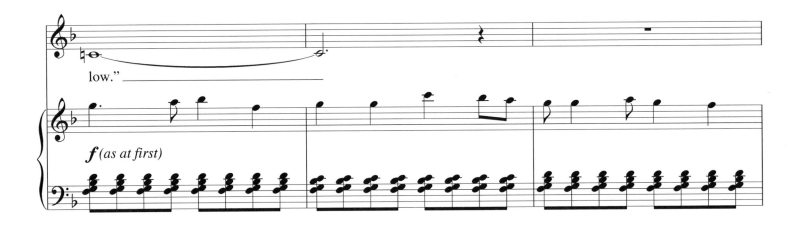

low." _____

f (as at first)

p

"If it was-n't for the love that I have for your men, I'd

(*p*)

do un-to you as I done un-to them, I'd sink you in the low -

8va --------------

(*mp*)

(*poco accentuàto*)

bot - tom of the sea. _____ Sank him -

self ___ in the low - land lone - some low, Sank him - self ___ in the

land that lies so low. _____

(molto cresc.)

4. AT THE RIVER
(Hymn Tune)
original key: E♭ Major

Arranged by
AARON COPLAND

Shall we gath-er by the riv - er, Where bright an-gels feet have trod, _____ With its crys-tal tide for- ev - er Flow-ing by the __ throne of __ God.

Yes we'll __ gath-er by the riv - er, the beau-ti-ful, the beau-ti-ful __

With dignity

poco cresc.

sub. p

river, Gather with the saints __ by the riv - er That

flows by the throne of __ God. __

cresc.

ff

Soon we'll reach the shin - ing

(cresc.)

ff

meno f

river, Soon our pil-grim-age will cease, __

meno f

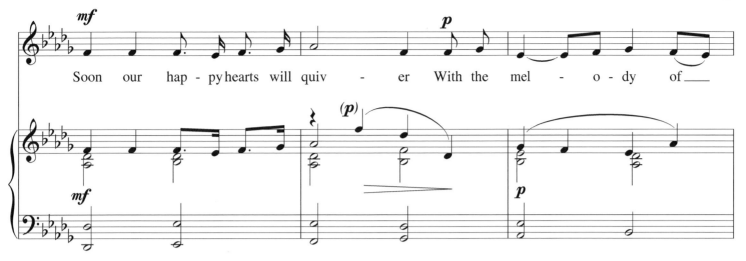

Soon our hap-py hearts will quiv - er With the mel - o - dy of ___

peace. Yes we'll ___ gath-er by the riv - er, The

beau - ti - ful, the beau - ti - ful ___ riv - er, Gath - er with the saints ___ by the

riv - er That flows by the throne of ___ God, ___ That flows by the throne of ___ God.

5. CHING-A-RING CHAW

(Minstrel Song)

original key: D Major

Arranged by
AARON COPLAND

Lively tempo (*with bounce*)
(*to be played with a light, sharp staccato throughout*)

Ching-a-ring-a ring ching ching, Ho - a ding-a ding kum lar - kee,

Ching-a-ring-a ring ching ching, Ho - a ding kum lar - kee.

Broth - ers ga - ther round, Lis - ten to this

52

fid - dle, Waltz and jig and prance, "Cast off down the mid - dle." _____

When the morn - in' come,

All in grand and splen - dour, Stand out in the sun, and

hear the ho - ly thun - der. _____